Trombone

HYMNS FOR BRASS

arranged for brass quintet
by Rick Walters

easy level

THE CANADIAN BRASS

CANADIAN
BRASS
SERIES OF
COLLECTED QUINTETS

2

Ah, Holy Jesus

TROMBONE

Johannes Crüger
("Herzliebster Jesu")

Christ the Lord is Risen Today

TROMBONE

from *Lyra Davidica,* 1708

Eternal Father, Strong to Save

TROMBONE

John B. Dykes, c. 1861

Beautiful Savior

TROMBONE

Silesian Melody
(Schönster Herr Jesu)

A Mighty Fortress

TROMBONE

Martin Luther, 1529

We Gather Together

TROMBONE

Netherlands Folk Song, 1626

C A N A D I A N   B R A S S
SERIES OF
COLLECTED QUINTETS

HYMNS FOR BRASS

arranged for brass quintet
by Rick Walters

contents

Welcome to the new *Canadian Brass Series of Collected Quintets*. In our work with students we have for some time been aware of the need for more brass quintet music at easy and intermediate levels of difficulty. We are continually observing a kind of "Renaissance" in brass music, not only in audience responses to our quintet, but to all brass music in general. The brass quintet, as a chamber ensemble, seems to have become as standard a chamber combination as a string quartet. That could not have been said twenty-five years ago. Brass quintets are popping up everywhere — professional quintets, junior and senior high school ensembles, college and university groups, and amateur quintets of adult players.

We have carefully chosen the literature for these collected quintets, and closely supervised the arrangements. Our aim was to retain a Canadian Brass flavor to each arrangement, and create attractive repertory designed so that any brass quintet can play it with satisfying results. We've often remarked to one another that we certainly wish that we'd had quintet arrangements like these when we were students!

Happy playing to you and your quintet.

— THE CANADIAN BRASS

U.S. $8.99

0-73999-88757-0

ISBN 978-1-4584-0157-1

50899

HL50488757

HAL•LEONARD®
CORPORATION
7777 W. BLUEMOUND RD. P.O. BOX 13819 MILWAUKEE, WI 53213